MW01100721

The Baskets of Baghdad

Poems of the Middle East

by Stanley K. Freiberg

including "The Lost List," a requiem story of the First Gulf War

and "Kindergarten to Iraq," an essay in verse

Newport Bay Publishing Limited, Victoria, British Columbia

Library and Archives Canada Cataloguing in Publication

Freiberg, Stanley K.
    The baskets of Baghdad : poems of the Middle East / Stanley K. Freiberg.

ISBN 0-921513-16-X

    1. Arab countries--Poetry. 2. Iraq War, 2003- --Poetry. I. Title.

PS3556.R46B3 2006   811'.54   C2006-902228-3

        Newport Bay Publishing Limited
        356 Cyril Owen Place
        R.R. 3, Victoria, B.C.
        Canada   V8X 3X1

International Standard Book Number 0-921513-16-X
Cover art: Catherine Doyle
Printed in Canada.

Table of Contents

Table of Contents (A-Z)

Dedication

This volume is gratefully dedicated
to
Students of the Class of 1966
of the
College of Education
University of Baghdad
and
in memoriam to
Professors Ruth Wallerstein
and
Helen C. White
of the University of Wisconsin

Wars and Rumors of Wars
are the Clarion Calls
of Infected Vision

"Beauty will save
the world,"—

– Dostoyevsky

Foreword

This reprinted edition of selected Middle East poems (1967) is
rededicated to my cherished students of the 1964-5 school
year at the University of Baghdad and to my University of
Wisconsin teachers Helen White and Ruth Wallerstein who
made the work possible.

The short story "The Lost List" is a requiem to students,
friends and neighbors who suffered and died in the 1991 Iraq
war.

The "Kindergarten to Iraq" work presumes to be a historical,
cultural, literary essay in poetry and prose on the 2003
invasion of Iraq by empire and religion wrapped in war.
Special thanks is extended to vocalist Dawna Beach for her
presentation of the volume's title poem *Once in Louisiana* at
the Victoria Conservatory of Music on November 15, 2004;
and to the cast of the author's play *Bush, Blake & Job in the
Garden of Eden*, performed in Victoria, B.C. on September 9,
2005.

- SKF

Once in Louisiana

Once in Louisiana, long ago,
I walked at evening on a gravel road
That stretched forever toward
                    the sinking sun.

Not a tree, not a bird,
Nor any colored stone
        do I remember now —
But only that I was alone
At sundown on an empty road.

Today the ageless sun swings down
                    toward Abu Ghraib,
An old Iraqi town;
And on this roadway to the west,
I wonder where the years have gone,
And if I still am walking on
Louisiana stone.

Once in Louisiana

Words and Music by Stanley Freiberg
Arranged by Tim Plait

down   toward A - bu   Graib,   an old I - raq - i   town.

And on this road - way to the   west,   I won - der where the years have

gone,   and if I   still   am walk - ing   on   Lou - is - i - a - na

stone.

IRAQ

Calm of the bone,
Patience of blood is the touch of this land.
Brown children, barefoot,
   walk noiseless through the silt-soft soil;
Sheep, stepless, nod where shepherds lean,
Statues on staves;
Women move with headborne baskets gracefully.
Palms sear eternally in windless air;
Fields, birdless, sleep the sands
          of dry antiquity.

The Tigris flows forever in the sun,
With unremitting movement of the veins
Along the dust-carved marrow of the bone.

Where Once My Father Walked

Once was a garden, gold and green,
                where every pleasant, fruitful tree
Took root; where waters four-fold,
In full flood, spilled steadily.
These were the trees
                where once my father walked,
As I in youth,
Upon the cool, eternal grass,
Shaded from truth: —
Hid from the dawns of desolation
That blasted green beginnings
                with bleak dust; --
Singing with shepherds long before
                the cities waked;
Walking the silence of the hills
Where wheels surprised the camel's path;
Bathing in fresh, immortal streams
                before the rivers dried.

Now are these times of Adam old
Slipped back beyond remembering;
The days between are blurred and dimmed,
Like dreams at waking, partly gone —
And I am in strange cities lost,
Divided from my certainties
Where children play with Eden in their eyes.

Babylon

Past buried palaces, cold in the sun,
Euphrates flows.
No chariots stallion through the wheel-churned dust;
No swaying galley carves the mirrored calm;
No towers grace green gardens tall with trees;
No silks are rustled in the nightfall breeze.
The nymphs have all departed
With the singing and the gold of Babylon.

Transformed,
They kneel at washing by brown shores
    where cattle stand like questions in the mire.
They gossip in cramped markets filled with flies;
Herd sheep and children through cart-crowded streets;
Cook gruel in blackened hovels made of clay.
At night they dream upon the callous ground
Of seven years of madness crawling back
Through fields of mud and owls and bats
Until they reach the gates of song and gold.

The Baskets of Baghdad

Upon the rainbowed bridges of Baghdad,
Brimmed baskets, balanced carefully
Above black abas flowing free,
Glide through thick crowds, responsibly.
Here are some curving fish
Swimming on ice in a dish;
And here some peppers, red and green,
Mixed with peeled onions, white and clean;
Rose pomegranates and yellow pears
Piled high like beaded palace stairs;
Some frightened chickens, staring down
To make a feathered jewel-eyed crown.
Melons striped and shimmering grapes,
Heaps of eggs and mounds of dates,
Leban, biscuits, nuts, and bread
All ride in state upon the head.

       Brimming baskets lifted high
       Raise rainbowed bridges in the sky.

Man and Stones

At dawn he stood at loading
                    like a beast
Beside a mound of stones
                    in Rashid Street.
Around his forehead twisted bands
Secured a burlap sling upon his back.
By time-scraped hands
            the sack was filled,
Until the crushing circle was his world.

Through honking hoofbeats and humanity
He labored till the turn to Shuhada.*
Then lifting up his eyes
            he saw the Martyr's Bridge
Arch toward the sky.
He set his face toward earth and mounted up,
And as he toiled
Great beads of sweat coursed round
                    his cutting crown.
The burden of the desert pressed his bone.
  No one, though on the road to Golgotha,
  Dare give his cross to this eternal man.

---

* The Martyr's Square on the south shore of the Tigris River

The Carter

Up Ahrar bridge there came a cart
   piled high with cartons of red apples
      and sweet pears from Lebanon.
The leathered Carter, thin, with calves of steel,
Leaned his whole life into the turning wheel;
But as he climbed the circle of the arch
His pace was slackened, deadened, —
He could not reach the cruel, round top.
He stared, bewildered, that the cart should stop.
A gasping terror clutched his heaving chest;
A panic came into his clouding eyes.
   He hid his pain-scarred face from passersby;
   But there was no escaping from the sun.
   He took his fruit-filled boxes one by one
   And set them down like lost years on the ground.

Shuhada Square

Meat pies, mirrors, pencils, milk,
  are all for sale in Shuhada,
The square where eccentricity
  has gained the name of normalcy;
The square where beggars, buses, porters,
Vendors, donkeys, cars, police,
Commuters, camels, tourists, sheep,
Congregate on every morning
      of the busy Baghdad week.
Yet the man I saw one morning
      was not of the common herd:
Aladdin-like he had the genius
      to gain notoriety —
To be different in a crowd
      of infinite variety.
Buying, selling, going, coming,
Were as nothing to this man.
He was standing on a large box
      on an island in the street,
Singing to the jogging horses —
To anyone he chanced to meet,
Those who passed him, passed with laughter,
But he sang on heedlessly;
Sometimes, though, he interrupted
      to give a short soliloquy.
Stepping down from his high station,

He strolled about with nonchalance;
Then suddenly, with kick of heels,
He broke into a joyous dance.
Resting on his box with pleasure,
He blew white smoke rings with a smile.
When the shurta came to take him,
Shuhada lost part of its style.

Twin Reality

Thin haze had put a halo round the sun
   when over Ahrar bridge there came
A twin reality, passing like a double dream
Resisting separation:
Upon the bridge there creaked
                    a horse drawn cart,
Piled high with fresh-dug sod
Grown over with long blades of green;
And on the grasses lay
                    a sleeping man,
His scarf and robes caught by the breeze,
A shovel at his side.
So sound he slept in his green bed
It seemed he had arrived in the Elysian fields,
And I in smiling at his bliss
Wished without fear that he might sleep eternally.

Before the cart had reached the further shore,
There came an endless caravan of death
In solemn passage to the holy south.*
Lashed crosswise, crucified,
Upon a car top, shining black,

A coffin, mummy shaped,
              an aba for a winding sheet;**
Led grief's procession stretching back
              beyond the turn to Rashid Street.
A hush fell on death's moving robe
Which, like a vision brought into the day,
Passed slowly through the faces of the crowd.
The silence uttered all my fears aloud,
For this was joyless sleep that could not wake.

---

* Moslems are often buried south of Baghdad in the holy cities of
Karbala, Najaf, and Kufa.
** The outer garment of Moslem women, worn daily, is often wrapped,
at death, around the coffin.

Woman and Child

Morning was at her back
As she sat tented underneath
                  her aba black.
She was a mound of coal,
A mass of threadbare pitch.
Even the hand that clutched the dish
                  of her small dreams
Was wrapped in night.

Beside her sat a lively boy,
                  with laughing eyes,
Who watched the swelling crowd
                  stream with the yellow sun
Down Ahrar bridge into the heart of day.
No dish had he.
Cradling cool feet like comfort in his hands,
                  he rocked and smiled.
But all the while the sackcloth tent beside him
                  never stirred.

To most among the waking crowd,
                  who passed them by,
One was invisible.

Day's Shadow

White hot, the sun slides toward the sea of time;
Listless and pale, an early moon begins to climb
        into the apathetic, ash-white atmosphere.
The suffocated breeze sifts down
        like feathers sent from dying birds.
The landscape is a haze of breathless gray.
Silence and heat lie motionless
        upon the burnt sarcophagus of day.

Now camels, noiseless, from the desert come.
On giant feet in droves
        they drift above the housetops steadily.
Humped higher than the moon,
        they tread the twilight in swift strides,
        more solemn than the bloodless air.
Into the east they move, methodically,
Gaunt figures numberless, a countless caravan
        of leathered phantoms, riderless —
Somber fugitives moving steadily
           seeking cool stars.

The Shovelers

Along the road that runs
> to Abu Ghraib
The shovelers wait.
Garbed in gray gowns
> and agals turbaned round,
They lean like herdsmen
> on their bladed staves.
When rumbling loads
> of gravel hesitate,
They toss their anxious crooks
> up sandy heights
And clamber after like blown sheets
> in nervous joy.
Away upon their cargoes
> of success
They ride like children
> grown too old to sing,
While at the roadside
> those they left behind
Shift back to ancient postures
> in the sun.
Day-long the handle rubs
> the shoulder raw,

And probes in silence
          at the vacant sky.
Day-long the dust-choked road
                roars heedless by
Where waiting limbs
          squat stoically.

On into dark they wait,
Some sleeping on the ground,
Some sitting by small fires,
Like shepherds keeping watch
Of flocks by night.
But round about
      stretch lonely fields of clay.
The roadway empty lies.
The sounds of day-long unsuccess
Echo in the midnight skies.

Ahl as-Sarifa

Ahl as-Sarifa, people of the mudhuts,
I have seen your dwellings
Stretch like endless honeycombs
          brown in the sun.
I have seen them also
       single in the fields,
One by one.
In clusters through the city,
At the turning past tall gates,
Near crumbling walls
       and ditches dank,
And on the reed grown riverbank,
       you set your clay.

I have walked past your houses
    at the dawning of the day,
When from great pans
      upon their heads
Your wives winnow the grain,
Spilling it down through sunshafts
Like gold rain toward the ground.

I have walked past at noontide
      when the houses are asleep,
When the donkey droops beside the wall
    and the shade is filled with sheep.

At evening I have seen you,
When your talks in the twilight are done,
Lighting your lamps in dark doorways
                and vanishing
                    one by one.

    Were I to gaze in the moonlight,
    Where time-worn grotesque shadows lay,
    What more would I know at the dawning
    Of your ancient, inscrutable clay?

Moslem in the Fields

Beneath the searing sun of breathless noon,
A figure, loose-robed, hoes incessantly.
Thin dust smokes up along the scorching soil,
White sky burns on bent shoulders steadfastly.

Tall as a man, upon a hand-hewn stick,
The only other figure in the field,
A flag of faith in solid green hangs motionless,
                    engraved upon the noontide air.

All day, through centuries long, they have been there,
This steadfast, unremitting, wedded pair:
The man who moves forever down the rows;
The green that from the dust forever grows.

Trinity

Great sheaves of green
                    bulged from the donkey's sides;
His white neck jogged persistence
                    under rain-washed skies.
Upon his back there rode a limber boy
                    with sober eyes;
And with the pair,
A black-robed woman limped
                    upon sharp stones of enterprise.
Each gate bell rang beneath her fingers lean;
Each market heard her pleading whispers thin;
Until in fading hours of afternoon
She mounted where the precious sheaves had been.
Caught in the circle of the setting sun
                    these simple figures journeyed, three in one.

Circling Birds

Stiff-necked, a turbaned head jerked twice
        above a polished cane of ebony,
And in the waiting bus there came a gentleman
            in business black.
Straight-backed, upon the first seat's edge
He perched, as if he were the only passenger
        and his arrival signified, "Begin!"
He paused a moment, dazed at the delay;
Then, taking out his watch, he gazed in pain.
He made a bruffing noise of discontent;
Then looked arm's length upon his watch again.
Soon he began a muttering to himself,
        and as he snorted in his discontent,
He held a string of beautiful black beads
    and fingered them with fever in his veins.

Above the North Gate mosque dome,
         blue and gold,
The storks in circles floated, smooth, serene.
Long necks stretched out in lines against the sky
Like swift white arrows, targetless.
Wings, motionless, sent whirling minarets
      of spiraled necklaces in graceful glides
          through waves of blue.

Below the circling of the silent birds
    that soar above the churches all day long,
Red buses chug and snort like angry men;
Impatient watches mark the restless hours.

The Golden Mosque

Brown is the land that lies above Baghdad
Upon the level road to Samarra.
Here smoke stacks, like dark idols
                        scrape dull sky;
And heat-glazed men feed furnaces with straw
To cure the countless bricks that shape the cities.

Beyond this noon-dark plain of smoke and toil,
In distant days, Baghdad's Caliph Al-Mutasin
Built a towering minaret of bricks at Samarra
                for prayers and festive seasons.

But chimneys charred and bricks and ceaseless toil
Longed for some transcendent beauty in the sky.

Skilled goldsmiths, in pits of flaming holy fire,
Blended the sun itself into burnished foil.
Samarra's Al-Askariya mosque was lifted into heaven,
                above earth's darkling plain,
            in curving songs of hammered gold.

Caliph Al-Mutasin's minaret at Samarra was constructed in 836 A.D.

The Long Miles

Narrow gauge, steel rails stretch
North toward Mosul, the high hills
                    and the green grain,
South toward Basrah, the date palms
                    and the swift ships.
Between lie the long miles,
The brown land, the marshes,
The shepherds, the gleaners.

Work trains with gray-robed workers
                    riding on flat cars,
Camel the long miles steadily
Through sun-white, heat-charred afternoons;
Through silent, cooling midnight stars.

Hospitality

Down from the furthest, cooling stars
The desert breezes come
                    like soothing voices
                    singing in the dark,
Lulling the fevered sands to sleep;
And in the distance
          an open doorway shines
Like hospitality
          born in the midst of isolation.
By lamplight
    will the midnight keeper bring
Fresh water from his earthen jar,
Hot hamuth from his flame of oil.
Wordless will he
    bring comfort in thin cups
And gather meager fils
    with time-scarred hands.
No traveler scanning stars
                    in desert dark
Will miss the yellow light
                    of his small door.

Impression of Evening

Walking at evening
                    where the donkey's feet
Have cut into the soil all day long,
Walking at evening
                    where the sun
Sinks like a tiny circle in the sand,
A longing lurks in silhouettes.
The gentle pain of passing time invests the air.
Small, songless birds of evening rise
As stillness vanquishes despair.
The twilight lifts insensate stars
                    into the circle of the night,
And all the paths of flesh and bone
Send silent shadows of surrender
                    to the sun.

Lovers' Ghosts

Before the clock struck twelve in Sadoun Street,
Her heels clicked out the rhythm of defeat.
She hung her only nylons on a chair
And in the darkness, on her iron bed,
Resigned her plight to sobbing and despair.

Above her coughed an ancient, dying crone,
A miracle of breath, encased in bone.
Below her reeked the urine-encrusted walls
Where mini-skirted anguish lingered.

Around her lurked the hooded, lusting dark
That pressed her thighs like lovers' ghosts.
She lay in loneliness, with nightmare scenes
Of cobweb stockings spun
                    by skeletons.

Woman of the Basrah Streets

Old woman of the Basrah Streets,
Ragged as a scarecrow, foolish as a clown,
Why do you come back every day
To act your tragedy
        before the teeth of grim hilarity?
I see the young men spin you round
                to watch the comedy
Of grime-ground feet splay awkwardly
Beneath the filthy rags of aged distress.
Now this one bows
        before his comic queen,
While one unveils the face you wept
                when you were yet a child.
They praise your beauty, ask you for a kiss,
And urge you mockingly to satisfy desire.

Why, old woman of the streets,
                do you come back each day
To dance where torment courts
                and pain is king?
To be the laughter of the purblind crowd?
What folly brings you limping, toothless toward
The acting of a part you cannot know?
Or are you wiser than we fools
Who, face deformed and feet decayed,
Give up the dance and every hope of love?

No Tales of Arcady

The figure Rodin carved in bending thought
Decays before this ancient sidewalk shop.
An empty cheek lies in a sun-dried hand.
His eyes have crept away, far from the light.
Behind him lies the craft of his long day:
Green vessels, single-shaped, and made of clay—
No figures in pursuit, no maidens loath,
No tales of Tempe or of Arcady.

      All day he sits face down beneath the sun,
      Engraved upon art's exile like a wound.

Alms

The oleanders, blooming pink and white,
Are tall enough to bend above low walls
        along the sidewalks in Waziriah.
One spot there is of dappled sun and shade
Where an old man often comes
        to warm himself and say his beads.
He puts his shoes upon the wall quite far away.
Why he removes them no one can quite say.
Perhaps it is a penitential act,
      or comfort may be it — simple as that.
At any rate,
One day a tiny girl, who thought
        they were for alms,
Came timidly
      to fill those empty shoes
          with fresh-picked flowers.

A Wall in Hilla

There is a wall in Hilla,
                    scarred and brown,
Low and crumbling,
                    where sellers bring small wares:
Trinkets, beads and baskets;
Some with tea and biscuits;
Old crones with chickens
                    nursing heaps of grain.
And one who neither sees the gold-haired sun,
Nor hears the street go echoing down the years.
He pleads in silence with his prayer-cupped hands,
While up in olive trees behind the wall
Birds flutter silently in silver leaves.

Oh, that one morning he might mount the sky
To sing with birds and perch in olive trees
To watch a feather falling silently
   upon his neighbors gathered on the ground.

Still Does He Sing

Through bitter dawns, December's curse,
And all the days of blighting summer dust,
He sits and sings.
His back humped up against his wailing wall,
He chants his plea for alms in Allah's name.
His Mecca is the multitude
He faces with his outstretched, palsied hand.
His music is a mournful cry
                of blessing for the merciful and good:
"May Allah bless you,
You who help my pain;
May you, your house and children
Escape harm."

Day of Dust

Upon a day of drifting dust
The light fell down, decayed at dawn;
The jaundiced mosques and bridges rose
Like phantoms in the stifling air.
Filled with substantial, ghostly gray,
The city knew no emptiness;
No space existed, and the streets
Were moving, half-screened tapestries
                              outlined in dust.
Thin, shrouded figures met in secret places,
Sent swirling sounds into the shifting void,
Then hovered, dwindled, disappeared,
Like floating particles of dying dreams.

Day-long, questing, displaced, unlaid faces
Left soft silt traces
                    where their apparitions moved.

Latent Images

Grim fog fills gray, cold morning specter full.
Vague, black-robed women
Sift noiseless through the photographic air.
Upon the negative of pale, bleak dawn,
Swart, shifting shapes reverse the witching hour.
Like frozen dreams, the eucalyptus leans,
        engraved upon the insubstantial light;
The willow, hanging limp and colorless,
Seems pathos bending down
                    toward outlined lambs;
Square misty shoulders of the city shrug
Like rugged problems sent to cloudy rooms
                    and unknown places.
Reduced to latent images,
The landscape yearns for vanished glimpses
                of its age-old sun.

By Babylon's Shores

Village of Babylon,
Brown on the banks of green Euphrates,
                   flowing free,
Your watchdogs guard old streets
                        near ancient ruins.
Your water buffaloes, black in the sun,
Seem like the large encumbrances
                     of small estates.
Your women, in long rows,
At washing on the shore
                   talk earnestly,
As if at bringing secrets out of doors.
Across the flood,
      where donkeys circle endlessly,
There creaks the shaft
                of an old wooden well;
And all along the river's swirling course
Great palms fan high in groves of green.
      A stranger in the land,
      I sit down by Edenic shores
      To sing.
      Are these the selfsame waters
      Judah wept?

Tooth Pulling

Between the buses and the sidewalk shops,
Among the donkeys and the spinning carts,
Beside the rushing crowd, near honking cars,
Just off the sidewalk was — the dental chair.
Four dentists of small size were gathered there,
All dressed in gowns of candy stripe

                 — not too well sterilized —

All staring happily

         — and quite professionally —

             into the patient's eyes.
Though dressed as medically as his compeers,
The patient was some short in height and years.
Especially was he short on happiness.
He stood wide-mouthed before his aides in tears.
The tallest of the gay, consulting crew

     sobered to give a kindly word or two.
It was a noble effort at relief,

     for he himself was to be surgeon chief.
The first attempt was like an internship:
The patient moved, the doctor's fingers slipped.
But with a reprimand, all was corrected;
With stunning ease, the tooth was disconnected.

The four practitioners stared as struck dumb
           upon the tiny object of success;
The victor probed his losses with his tongue —
It felt like something gained and something less.
Now, suddenly, a wagon passing by
      seemed signal for the close of dentistry:
Swift togas scrambled up across the gate
And on the load sat five new men of state.

Coppersmith

Cups and chains and camels' bells
        are hammered out of sweat and fire
By this old coppersmith.
Waist-deep he stands within his dingy pit
And thrusts black tongs upon his roaring forge;
Then drawing red-gold metal from the flame
He hammers shapes held secret in his hand:
Curved vases rise like spring in quest of flowers;
Small dishes carry messages inlaid;
Bells molded with full throats, ring huskily;
Cups tinkle in thin copper, daintily.
With every object sent to test the light
The hammer sings a thunder in the wind,
As if fierce gods at fashioning firm worlds
Try beauty in the pits of flaming night.

Black Rocks of Jordan

Wide, interminable, the black rocks stretch
      like sinister companions, motionless.
No flower, no tree, no bird songs from the ground;
But only boulders dark, grotesque,
          and endless as eternity.
Amidst this hard, sharp chaos camels stroll
Like gaunt first forms of humped endurance
      walking through the void.
Sometimes the stones are heaped like altars strange,
Unvisited, placed by the gods themselves;
Sometimes, like livid scars,
The sun dried streams in twisting pain
      cut through the stubborn dark.
And once in every eon is a path
Dug out by unseen hands among the rocks.
Here camels black and brown, gray, gold and white
Graze on the green beginnings of the world

Bedouin Love Song

To the place where your father's tent stood,
I came at the waking dawn.
When the sun sent its wings up out of the east,
I came, but you were gone.
Over black rocks of the desert,
Over the wastes without trees,
Along dried streams and drifting dunes,
I came, but you were gone.

Where have you wandered, my cousin?
Where have you wandered, my love?
Where will I find your fair, dark eyes
I loved when you were a child?
Where will I see you walking,
Lovely, and proud, and wild?

Before we were pledged by our fathers,
I gave my whole heart away
That I might one day seek you
As I have come seeking today.
But where have you wandered, my cousin?
Where is your tent standing now?
Are you living among the black rocks,
Hoping I'll find you somehow?

I thought to joy at your beauty,
Curved in soft songs like the sun,
But here there is only wasteland,
Lonely and empty as pain.
Would that the dawn wind's low whisper
Were your voice calling my name,
Would that the falcon's uprising
Would lead me with wings to your home.
How shall I find you, my cousin?
How shall I find you, my love?
Why have you gone before sunrise
And left me the darkness of dawn?

Flight Into Egypt

At dawn I saw them rise out of the east,
A trinity of figures in the dust.
In robes of gray, before a jogging beast,
A strong-stepped man paced quickly
                        on his way.
Upon the donkey's back,
There rode a dark-eyed, limber girl
Wrapped round in black.
Such was their haste they seemed to flee
Across the desert to a foreign soil.
They passed so rapidly
I could not see
If in the woman's arms
There was a child.

And There Were Shepherds

We drove through fields of springtime
        in green curves
Through terraced hill sides up to Bethlehem.
Red poppies fringed the orchards like glad blood;
White daisies starred new grain
           like pure, round thoughts.
The resurrected landscape drifted by
Until we reached the summit in blue sky.
Then out of Bethlehem we walked a way,
Down,
        down, and to the east where lay
The shepherds' fields
    where once the angels sang.
Then we remembered winter and a star:
No flowered fields, but winds up in the dark.
No easy climb, but footsore faith uphill
Until they gained a stable cold as death,
Where swaddled spring
        was sleeping in the flesh.

The Carpenter's Son

Just as I smiled in friendship at the boy,
   scarce tall enough to reach the board he held,
He must have made some criminal mistake.
The father crushed his hand upon the face
With force enough to make the mind breathe pain.
Incredulous, the child wept.
Part of his heart was in the grave.
He was a statue, wishing not to grow.
But, once again, he took the burden up
And, blinded, started forward through the years.

Another day, all filled with rain
          and wind-blown skies,
I found the shop closed tight.
Its metal door seemed like a gloomy veil
Pulled down to hide
The ghosts of sorrow put to sleep inside.

Yet, when I passed it once again in spring,
The pair had paused together in the sun
To watch white doves of morning climb the sky.
The father touched the boy so tenderly,
He could not be the same who made him cry.

Sleeping Child

Karachi, Pakistan

Brown and beautiful
      in her blue dress,
The child slept
      beneath the shop shelves
Where her father kept his needlework,
Brass wares and hand-carved elephants.
White-robed, he sat beside her,
Sewing slowly, wrinkle-eyed,
Seeming to stitch contentment
      into their obscure lives.

It was the quiet time.
No shoppers crowded through
      the foot-scarred streets;
No motion of the sun betrayed eternity.
And then I chanced upon
      this Joseph and his child,
This mortal, deathless pair,
Sewing the soft, sweet threads
      of swift humanity;
Sleeping the guileless sleep
      of blue-gowned childhood,
Brown and beautiful.

Mother and Children

Each night she sits
                    like sorrow in the flesh,
                    like grief made manifest,
In Tahrir square,
Stretching her hand, still strong and fair,
                    out to the swirling multitude.
Beside her there,
As if upon an island for the small,
Four children sleep,
                        like cherubs on a rug,
As round them flow reluctant feet
                        of their salvation.

"Sadaqat! Sadaqat!"
Through slow, sad hours
                    she cries out steadily;
And even when the street
                    is only ghosts
She keeps her place.
Then four small figures rise
                    before her face
And cast long shadows
                    like the fully grown.
She drops her agèd, withered hand
                    into her lap
And sits alone.

Dome of the Rock

Beneath a dome of gold
Raised on the ancient soil
      where Solomon once walked
And all his riches were displayed,
There rests a rock,
Completely unadorned,
Except with its own whiteness
        and its abiding purity.
Above it Persian craft
    has carved the Koran's holiness
    in silver, gold, and amethyst,
Sending hallowed light
       down toward the stone.

Upon this rock, in faith and fear,
Obedient Abraham bound his son's flesh
And Allah's prophet placed his foot
      on his heavenward journey.
The portals of this shrine
      are circled by the shoes
Of Moslems, Gentiles, Jews,
Who leave these outward coverings
In the sun
To stand within the Vision
        where all humanity is one.

Harvest

Sweet is the morning air,
     breathing the fresh-cut fields,
     washed with the scent of rain.
Gray is the sky,
     except far down the east
     where sun shafts lie on clouds
       like unbound wheat.
Along a row of eucalyptus trees,
     Iraqi women bend in black
     above the tassled stalks
       of yellow grain,
Cutting with sickles sharp
     and hands as wrinkled as antiquity;
Binding with ceaseless care the
     sheaves of time
Beneath the mellow skies
     of ripening dawn.

Summer's End

The dawn wind blows a sharpness in the sun;
The river lifts soft vapor to the light;
White doves of morning shiver in the trees;
Dew lies in gold-chilled pebbles on the grass.

Now are the dawns of warning on Baghdad,
The signs of winter signaled in the sun.
Now women gather leaves of palm and sticks,
The drying camelthorn and sheaves of straw,
And bundle them in headborne loads.
Great round cakes of flat-pressed cattle dung
Are carried in tall towers through the streets;
Small chips and leaves in woven baskets ride
With solemn women, walking steadily.
　　　They lift the dying summer on their heads
　　　And carry it like hope toward coming cold.

Sorrow

Dressed in blue gowns and tan capes
                stretching down to sandaled feet,
With long scarves, gray and black,
                  wrapped round their heads,
These shepherds are the comfort of their sheep.
In certitude they pace before the flock
    or stand in watchful postures near the fringe.
Across the smitten dust of afternoon,
They lead lean ewes to stubble tall as joy
And ditches seeming fresh as Eden's streams.
At night they sit by fires upon the ground
    and sleep by turns within the circled light
To keep the jackal's tooth out in the dark.

At dawn they rise to new realities.
They lead the nervous flock through honking streets,
Across bowed bridges and through cart-filled crowds
    where lambs must be upgathered in their arms.
They clasp these children to their fearfilled breasts
And carry them toward slaughter through all harm.

Quiltmaker

See how he fluffs fresh cotton with his stick!
Quick tosses, snaps and whips
Until he sits surrounded by deep snow
     upon a summer's evening in Baghdad.
Now with a cover red and white
Spread out beneath dim yellow light,
His fingers thin move gracefully,
His soft, white mound melts magically,
And soon before delighted eyes
A quilt is padded, sewed and tied.
     Such movements deft and artful ways
     Deserve a kind of double praise,
     For he makes both a summer scene
     And patterns for warm winter dreams.

Hattaba *

With winter gone, there seemed no cause,
That as the twilight sun slipped down
                    in promise of a warmer dawn,
A kneeling woman, aged but strong,
Should stay at cutting wood against the light.
Had she not raised her adz so furiously,
One would have thought her at her evening prayer;
But she was set on gathering,
                    and stroke by stroke,
She laid the gnarled stump bare.
The sticks she gathered in the falling light
Were lifted like small children to her breast.
Toward silent silhouetted palms
She rose to take her burden to the west.

* Woman woodcutter.

The Winds of Winter

The winds of winter hiss across gray skies,
December sinks cold fangs into the flesh,
As throbbing through the cringing atmosphere
The imam's chant comes singing of bleak death.
No single center has his mournful voice,
But comes from south, north,

                    east and west.
We seem surrounded by his chilling breath.

To warm us in the middle of the dark,
We light a candle for the parting soul —
A gold reminder of the summer days
When shoulders felt the sweetness of the sun.

Through days and nights
The sacred chant of pilgrimage

               will fill the Mamoun skies,
And all the while the candle's flame

          will send its flickering answer toward

               the imam's cries.

Pilgrims

Rain pelts the Baghdad February clay
Until the city seems a mud-capped sea.
Solemn footsteps tread gray bricks
Amid brown buildings and bare trees.
The cloud-high mosques,

               with ornate figurings,

Are passed unseen by anxious, downcast eyes.
All move on ceaselessly,
As if upon their way

        to some known, strange,

              and far-off destination.

They seem like Bunyan's pilgrims on
Their way across the great Slough of Despond.

The Coves of Memory

Rising to meet her bridges
           arched toward dawn,
The city brings her flesh into the light.
Feet crowd gray streets above brown shores
           flown white with birds;
Hooves clatter toward crushed markets
           filled with hands.
The Tigris has come back into the day.
A time of shrinking, shivering in the north;
A time of dying slowly in its bed;
But now in eddies rich with crimson clay
         it rises up like passion in the veins.
The seed is singing in the anxious soil;
The birds are clapping in the leafing trees;
The lambs are bounding in the dew-fresh fields;
The clouds are leaping in the laughing skies.
The year revolves again.
The sutures of the heart heal suddenly
As seasons in the grass among the flowers
   call bird-like through the coves of memory.
The light stays longer in the red-gold west,
Brown girls sway pleasure in the lusting blood,
The musgouf cooks along the river front.
Soft, waking winds lift the eternal stars.

Last Flight to Eden

Now, before sunfail,
Before the birds of blackness
            raven in the night,
Before the spinning clock hand
            stabs the halting heart,
Whirl backward into noontide,
Fly eastward into dawn,
Walk through the garden golden
      where innocence was born.
Forget the bitter apple
      that God taught how to bite;
Remember Eve,
      soft, supple,
      her body brown delight.
Forget the coal-black serpent
      and paradise undone;
Remember Adam tranquil
      at the setting of the sun.
Recall that consummation
      before the birth of time
When pleasure was so passionate
      it moved without design.

Now wheel red eyes to westward
    where the hymen sun bleeds down
And feel day's desecrations
    like pythons in the groin.
For never was a harlot
    who was not virgin first,
And Mary is but naked Eve
    in nightgowns of the church.
And Adam Old is sleeping
    in the beds of Babylon
While the Cherub's sword is flaming
    and the sexless night comes on.

Retrospect

Before the stars were born,
We sang like morning
           choired in the east.
The tides and winds
                were chained,
Time unreleased.
With rounded, clustered songs
           our baskets brimmed,
With wine flow of desire
                our bodies burned.
The grape crushed in the mouth
                rushed like the sea,
Tempestuously.
No fangs of separation coiled
                near poison trees.

Joyful, at dawn, our hands
                touched gem-round dews,
Like new days cradled countless
                on the flowers.
Happy, in evening cool,
Our voices walked
           upon the holy hills
That could not fade.
No apple of decision
           forked our dreams;

The tides and winds were still —-
        unheard, unseen.

Subtle, Time's serpent slid
Into the garden
        of our innocence,
Shedding the past
        in silk-soft sheaths,
Winding the clock
        in wine-dark leaves.

Care coiled about the grape
And spewed the emptied flesh
        upon the ground.
Our separate fears
        ticked in our ribs
Like destiny, unbound.
Rough waves curled biting
        through red rocks.
Wild winds whirled darkly
        through Time's Tree
Of Mystery.

Night's Shadow

Twilight in crimson burns
                    on earth's curved edge,
Charring the rim-strewn palms
                    to silhouettes.
Sanguine, the roadway stretches
                    to the west.
Swart figures move like secrets
                    through red air.
Sequestered shadows ink
                    vermilion sands;
Flamed pools hold bending sheep
                    in sculptured time.
Beside his carven flock,
                    a shepherd stands,
Breathing his pipe to ashes
                    as the road
Darkens to but a ribbon in the mind.

Departure

The viscount whines a silver in the sun.
Brown land slips backward like the loss of time.
White, hot light bounces in on puzzled eyes.
Fleet, roaring wings bird into morning skies.
    Would that the heart were strong
          as these cruel wings
       that lift me from the soil of my songs!
Now Homer's eyes alone I need to see
The city spread beneath me like a flower;
The mind moves dovelike down to every tree
In benediction at this sacred hour.
The past is fleeing to the world of dream.
The future stretches toward the cloudless void.
The present lifts its holy hand and dies
Marking this separation in the skies.

Somewhere among those bricks and star-shaped
palms,
Upon arched bridges and through crowded streets,
In desert heat and chilling winter's rain,
The feet of those I love will walk the years;
And I may never see a single one.
    The viscount sings a sorrow in the sun.

The Lost List

Recollections and a Requiem
The Gulf War of 1991

An early morning rain, fresh and inviting, was falling softly, almost secretly, in Victoria. It was the dormant, damp, often mild season when long dead leaves of summer creep forth from hidden places like substantial ghosts to lie in the rain. The spring-like air curled beneath Elizabeth Simms' umbrella and brushed her face; but she walked numbly through the soft thin silk of the rain, feeling apprehensive and helpless.

Her mind was in Baghdad — a city sacred to her through long years -- and this was the day, almost certainly, that it would be bombed. During a school year long ago, brown, beautiful faces had watched her almost worshipfully, listening to her talk about Shakespeare and Keats and Hardy. Now she knew the streets of Baghdad were filled with panic and fear, not with noisy cars and creaking carts, occasional camels, flocks of sheep, busy voices and hurrying feet.

With downcast eyes, she walked slowly, solemnly along the deserted avenue toward the Blethering Tea Shop a few blocks from her cottage. A ragged piece of paper, tangled in a cluster of leaves along the curb, caught her eye. Her first inclination was to pick it up, not so much out of curiosity as from a vague desire to remove a kind of intruder or blemish from the world of the rain. She dismissed the impulse and went on to the tea shop where she often began her mornings.

Glaring headlines in newspapers in the foyer heightened her distress: "Americans Poised to Bomb

Iraq; Desert Storm to Be Unleashed." She felt vacant and chilled, fearing to visualize what was going to happen on the soil and to the people she loved. Her days in Baghdad had been exotic; exhilarating, and magical — days so precious they could never be lost.

Every day of the school year she had traveled from Mamoun on the outskirts of Baghdad across town to Waziria to teach at the university. Looking down from the upper deck of a red British-style bus, she delighted in the colourful chaos of carters and cars, countless kiosks and crowds, sidewalk vendors, and headborne baskets of fish, leban and fruit. She was at home in the city, "happy as the day was long."

Whenever she missed her bus and crowded into a taxi, there were deferential smiles — always attempts to exchange some words beyond simple greetings and goodbyes.

Whether traveling by bus or taxi, Elizabeth had to transfer at the Martyrs Square, one of the busiest interchanges in Baghdad. Buses, taxis and commuters congregated and departed in continuous waves, filling the very air with the feeling of imperative destinations. Elizabeth was at one with the crowd, anxiously waiting for a bus, or flagging a taxi.

The shrill calls of vendors punctuated the heavy chug and exhaust of the engines. On an island in the middle of the square, soapbox orators directed unheeded messages to the bustling parade of passers-by.

Elizabeth crossed the Tigris every school day over the Martyrs Bridge. When she returned home at evening, she sometimes took another route, wishing to look at the city from a different rainbowed bridge. Crossing the placid river, she was immortal, a wonder-filled child, surrounded by Eden alive and ancient, riding back and forth over the waters of the beginning oblivious to time's swift passing and the sovereign might of melancholy.

Seated at tea, she looked out intently at the rain-washed street, trying to dismiss her fears. Her thoughts turned back to the water-soaked scrap of paper she had seen. A strange restlessness came with the recollection. She felt oddly possessed by the notion that a list of some extraordinary significance was scribbled on the paper and that it had something to do with her.

She chided herself. She was overtired. Her night had been nearly sleepless, her worries about the war constant; so her mind had drifted into irrational assumptions over a discarded or lost piece of paper. Still, she was unable to entirely suppress conjectures about it. She wondered what, if anything, was written upon it and who might have lost it.

She recalled Granny Weatherall in K.A. Porter's story saying, "It's bitter to lose things!" and nodded in decided agreement. Then she smiled inwardly for allowing the supposed list to taunt and tease her as if she herself had actually misplaced something.

But the matter was not closed. On the way back to her cottage, Elizabeth saw an elderly man near the spot where she had seen the list. She felt certain that she saw him bend down and pick it up although she was quite some distance away and could not be absolutely certain. The man disappeared from her view, turning the corner into Clive Street. When she arrived with a twinge of anxiety at the spot where she had seen the paper, it had, like the man, disappeared.

She felt irritated — cheated! The man had somehow impinged upon or even trespassed upon her territory. Then she caught herself a second time and actually laughed aloud at herself in the empty street. Hadn't she, after all, nearly picked up the piece of paper? Why begrudge anyone who had felt the same inclination? Perhaps a list of some kind belonged to him. What difference could it possibly make if it didn't?

At home, the list evaporated from her thoughts. She was drawn to the continuous dispatches of impending war — the uncompromising resolution of the United States to "storm" the desert and bomb Baghdad. She shuddered at the specious rhetoric of war — civilians would be in relatively small danger; no harm was meant to the Iraqi people. When she heard reports that installations to the west of Baghdad were considered to be prime targets, her fears became even more intense and vivid.

She had lived with her husband in Mamoun, a suburb west of town. The district was a mélange of moderately large brick houses, tin-walled shops, and open areas where chickens and sheep wandered about in brown dust and niggardly vegetation.

The house that Elizabeth and her husband rented was a tall brick structure with a walled-in garden, located within sight of the highway leading to the west — to the College of Agriculture at Abu Graib; to the vast dust-blown desert and the black rocks of Jordan; to Amman and Jerusalem and Damascus.

Elizabeth had no idea what was meant by military installations; but she visualized the whole district between Mamoun and Abu Graib as having been expanded into a target area for U.S. bombers.

She was torn by an irrational anxiety for the house she had lived in and for the agricultural school where her husband had taught. Most of all, she feared for her neighbors who were engraved unchanged in her memory — the rotund, cheerful shopkeeper Jassim, still trying to teach her Arabic as he learned English; the lad Ayad from next door, bringing gifts almost every day of delicious flat bread, along with fly-ridden yogurt; the kerosene man with his donkey-drawn wagon, surrounded by children; familiar bus and taxi drivers slowing down forever where she waited every morning on her way to work. It was as if the threatened war caught and sealed her back in time, even as she had been caught up in a timeless existence while in Baghdad. Every trip through the city was exciting and eternal; every day in the classroom green and golden.

Nonetheless, she recalled her first days in the classroom with a mixture of amusement and pain. The variety she had seen in the Baghdad streets absolutely vanished. She walked into rooms filled with identical faces and forms. She could distinguish the sexes, of course; but in every classroom she found herself in the midst of look-alikes!

Not only identical in features, but in dress: all of the males in the same suits and ties; all of the females wearing the same jewelry and identical black mini-skirts. Her mind became a blur before a dark-eyed wave of brown faces; she herself stood shuddering on a distant shore — honey-blonde and self-consciously white.

Not being able to differentiate frightened and embarrassed her, and the same traumatic failure was repeated in all of her early meetings. Some consolation came from her husband Allen who, in his first classes, experienced the same confusion and fear.

Allen compared his dilemma with once having viewed a gallery of fascinating paintings by schizophrenics — the same intricate and complicated images reproduced exactingly over and over again.

Later, the two could recall those early days and laugh comfortably together, having quickly learned the names of all of their students. Shortly, it became a common practice to go with them on week-end excursions. They traveled to the Golden Mosque of Samarra, to the ruins of Babylon, to the Holy Cities of the South, to small villages on the banks of the Tigris and Euphrates.

At picnic time, a banquet of food miraculously appeared, placed upon tablecloths spread upon the ground — lamb and chicken, fruits and vegetables, flat bread and cheese, dolma and dates. There was singing and dancing and games, and always amusing spontaneous lessons in language.

In the bus everyone ate "hub" — pumpkin seeds, sunflower seeds, and pistachios. The husks were tossed, as if by communal obligation, on the floor. Singing in the bus was continuous, mostly in Arabic, but intermixed with snatches of English.

Echoes and visions and faces congealed and focused and floated through Elizabeth's mind. She had had some correspondence but seen no one from Baghdad through the years. Always there was the intention of revisiting Iraq, but time and circumstances intervened.

During and after the Iran-Iraq war, all contacts were
lost.

Elizabeth and Allen had managed to travel all the way
to Samarkand, but that was during the conflict
between Iran and Iraq. In Samarkand, the mosques
and markets, the dress and the language reminded
them of Iraq, and they longed to go to Baghdad. Even
after Allen's death, Elizabeth longed from time to time
to revisit Baghdad. Even now, at the moment of
impending conflict, she longed to be in her adopted
city. And her mind was there.

Throughout the day, she kept turning the television
off and on wishing to shut out the inevitable which
she knew she must face. She busied herself half-
heartedly at chores, tried to read, called her friend
Agnes next door several times.

The rain continued to fall all day, but in the late hours
of the afternoon became quite heavy. She looked out
at the gray skies and unrelenting rain as at an infinite
expanse of inexplicable despair.

Agnes came over soon after Elizabeth's third phone
call, sensing the mounting distress in her voice which
was characteristically calm and resonant. Tea and
biscuits were set while the two repeated snatches of
the concerned conversation exchanged on the phone.
Elizabeth sipped her tea, but was soon up pacing. She
carried her serviette and began twisting it in her
hands.

Agnes began to worry. She suggested that Elizabeth
take a sedative. Elizabeth was emphatic: she would
not! The culprits and the brainwashed needed
sedatives, not she! Agnes had never heard Elizabeth

speak in such a fashion. She suggested that they turn the TV off and take a walk in the rain.

Elizabeth did not want to walk in the rain. She had been walking in the rain all day! She had walked in the rain all her life!

Agnes knew very little about the symptoms of nervous exhaustion but felt Elizabeth was on the verge. She began to be greatly troubled, not knowing how to manage Elizabeth's comments and behaviour.

Suddenly, Elizabeth was kneeling in front of the television screen speaking derisively into the face of the newscaster. "Oh yes, of course, of course, they'll have to bomb the bridges! All of them, of course! The Northgate Bridge and the Second Bridge and Martyrs Bridge and the Southgate Bridge and the New Bridge — all of them! And they musn't forget to destroy my house and Bus 21; and to mutilate my sheep and chickens and camels and mosques and Mona and Farej, Abbas and Zahia, Majid and Nawal, Makia and Mohammed!" Her face was buried in her hands in a flood of hysterical tears. Agnes knelt beside her, weeping, trying to console her, not knowing what to say.

"Elizabeth! Elizabeth! It hasn't happened. Perhaps it won't happen. Please, come sit down. I think we should call Dr. Miller."

Elizabeth struggled to her feet, dizzy and nauseated. Agnes helped her to the divan.

No, Elizabeth didn't want Dr. Miller to be called. She wanted the television turned off. She would get hold of herself; she just needed a little rest. She'd stretch out on the divan, and after awhile, if she didn't feel better, they would call Dr. Miller.

Elizabeth was in her late sixties and had always been remarkably energetic and healthy; yet, the strain of the last several days had been constant and, finally, unbearable. It was as if her whole life were being undermined; as if she were being catapulted back into her youth and the joys she had cherished and nourished were about to be cruelly destroyed.

She turned to stone on the sofa, absolutely immobile; so much so that Agnes could scarcely see her breathing.

She breathed, or scarcely breathed, in Baghdad. She stood immobile, frozen, sculptured by the roadway, moveless as death, waiting for the bus from Abu Graib. Along the road before her, transfixed, wooden as toys, stretched a convoy of tanks and soldier-crammed trucks. No one, nothing stirred. The wind was whisperless, the desert without dust. No veil, black robe, or palm leaf fluttered. No carter, camel, boot, or pebble moved. All currents in the Tigris ceased; the sun was captured in its course, all time suspended. White flocks of storks above the North Gate Mosque were stilled in flight like painted ghosts upon the dome of heaven. The universe was carved in wax and stone, a single monument, motionless, fervorless, soundless, sealed in a timeless syncope. All movement was arrested and waited as in agony for some momentous signal to begin.

She knew if she should raise her hand the dreadful armistice with time would cease; the bus would come from Abu Graib, the convoy move, and every grain of sand be witness to untold calamity.

She would not move! She would not let one bird song rise up from the ground, the winds to breathe, the

Tigris to start flowing. She would prevent the advent of disaster by standing by the roadway fixed forever! She would not turn back toward her house to wave goodbye or ever board the bus again to cross the city to Waziria.

A tear coursed down her cheek and set the sun and moon in motion.

A whirlwind swallowed up the moments of stilled time! A great collision rocked the Martyrs Bridge and earthquaked through the world's foundations. The severed heads of screaming storks rained blood into the trembling river.

She ran in terror through the streets, rending her garments, crawling, raving, looking wildly for herself among the ruins; rushing from black-robed woman to black-robed woman beseeching everyone to give her back her child.

"Allah be praised, Allah be praised," echoed hollowly from headborne load to headborne load, from molten skies, from hidden passageways, from every stone, from widening fissures in the pavement.

She rushed down avenues of pain, frenzied, tormented, undone by the cruel ways of Allah, shouting, imploring, "Elizabeth! Elizabeth!"

The crater that devoured her was a whirling funnel — a vast, deep hourglass filling swiftly, inexorably with sand. Her body floated, swirled, and eddied among dismembered dolls, demented birds, and shards of fallen monuments.

Suddenly, the buoyant sands released her and she fell — headlong — through a narrow crevasse into the nether spaces of the universe. Through the dens of

Nightmare and her Ninefold, age after age, eon after eon, she fell the length of time into the smoke-filled, blackened smithy of primeval pain — stretched out upon an ancient anvil, wrapped in chains.

Agnes saw her stir and was relieved to see some movement; but Elizabeth was lying, in solitary vigil, upon a block of concrete beneath the broken girders of the Martyrs Bridge. The clamour and terror of armour and sirens had ceased; the feet of the living had drifted away through the twilight to vague destinations. Circled in sackcloth, a stoic moon had climbed the sky, whitening the great shattered bones of the bridge, broken and strewn in the river.

Elizabeth heard the waters washing about the desecrated fragments of the fallen bridge. The waters were crimson. The bodies of the slain floated and swirled in the debris of the bridge. No faces were familiar. In the moonlight and crimson no features were distinguishable, none different. All were brown leaves come secretly forth to lie in the Tigris at evening.

Elizabeth knew that the thin green-covered class book, in which she had written their names, floated somewhere among them; but it had been carried by merciless currents beyond the reach of her vision.

Voices

The war is behind us. We had no quarrel with the Iraqi people.

- George Bush

A voice is heard in Ramah, lamentation, and bitter weeping, Rachael weeping for her children ...

- Jeremiah xxxi, 15

... the communication
Of the dead is tongued with fire
beyond the language of the living.

- T.S.Eliot
Little Gidding

The city lay silent –
    the clamour and terror of sirens
        and armour had ceased;
    and mourners in twilight
        had drifted away
        to vague destinations.
I sat on a stone
    in the Square of the Martyrs
    and watched the moon rise.

Circled in sackcloth it rose,
    whitening the great shattered bones
        of the Bridge of the Martyrs,
    broken and strewn in the river.
Home to the Tigris at evening,
    the bodies of the slain
        washed and circled –
    floating, turning, swirling,
        decomposing
    in crimson oblations
        in the debris of the bridge.
They said no syllables.

Intaglio

(Upon seeing a picture in *Paris Match*)

"I betake me for refuge
to the Lord of the Daybreak,
Against the mischiefs of his creation."

- The Koran

Photographs are lies
    I half believe:
The past recalled; reality
        raked by the tines of time
        into enchanted fires;
        truth filtered, -
        faded, dimmed
        to thin, distorted light;
        white ashes waking
        in a night of dreams.
Photographs of scenes
        I have not looked upon
        with my own eyes
Are truly lies:
Witchproofs -
The alchemy
        of images still latent,
        remote and indistinct;

Synchromatic hoaxes
                    pretending that the aperture
                    of my own heart
                         let sunlight in.
This picture that you show me now
                    of Tahrir Square,*
                    seems like reality:
Though shadowed by the fall of time,
Half-trust awakes,
For once this palm-leaf circle
Seemed Eden to these very eyes.
But surely crones
                    who blow on knots**
Touched hands and breath
Upon the negative
That prints hanged men
In limp-doll postures
Around the garden fringes
Of this holy gate.
                    Neck-roped to death,
                    These bodies must be
                         etchings up from hell,
                    Suspended by some trick,
                    By dark-room magic,
                    Not by these human faces
                         in the crowd.

* South Gate Square in Baghdad, Iraq
** Weird women of mischief mentioned in The Koran

Kindergarten to Iraq

An Episodic Prose-Poem Essay

The kindergarten teacher's name was Miss Shepherd.
She had soft, silky blonde hair and soft, silky hands.
She sat with her children in a circle singing,
  "No boy knows when he goes to sleep."

Suddenly, she stood up and asked:
"Does the re-incarnated beetle know how distant
  or near his dark body is from rebirth or Nirvana?"

W. H. Auden was skipping rope in the doorway.
"To ask the hard question is simple," he said.

The two six-foot fifth grade Grendels
  were swallowing multi-colored marbles
    in the unfenced, sun-washed schoolyard.
Blue Angel fly-byes roared overhead and "America the
Beautiful"
  was sung before all major contests.

Eyes at the Franklin School window,
  in Eliot's cruel month,
    saw a spider suspended from the fire escape;
    bees content in foxglove bells;
      a treetop magnolia unfolding.

In that same moment, in his 29th of 80 years,
Gautama slid down the banister of his father's mansion,
        past the carved arms of Shiva,
           into the riddle of time.
At the foot of his garden, in a ditch,
  lay a nearly dead man,
        beaten, stripped and bleeding, fallen among
        thieves.

The rescue went well in Calcutta:
Guatama had CPR training;
      blankets and bandages rained down from heaven;
      Mother Teresa brought her donkey-drawn cart
        to carry the man to her convent.
      (She said nothing of doctrine or last rites
        to either her houseguest or Guatama.)

"Dogma betrayed" rattled Vatican windows
        and "sins of omission" the archives!
Garbed in the thunder and lightning of black
  and red gowns,
        occasionally celibate cardinals gathered
        to chastise, ponder penance, or even delay
Teresa on her way to fast-track, legendary
    Time Magazine cover,
        International- idol-saint fame.

Even more daunting—some or any notice,
        blessing or audience for a happenstance,

Hindu Samaritan, unbaptized and unaware of Rome's
  path to salvation?

A shade from Purgatory, with an underarm scroll,
        interrupted clandestine opinions.
He carried a relevant cold case 15th century CD
            of the Harrowing of Hell:
    "When the Saviour entered Hell with John the Baptist
    to release those who had lived worthily before
        His coming,
    the voices of the multitudes confined in darkness,
        rose as one,
    saying, 'What is this glorious light that shines so
        fairly over us?'

The Baptist was their well-prepared advocate
            for mercy and redemption.
He carried a scroll containing Torah and Biblical CVs.

Adam and Abraham, Isaac and Jacob, Moses
      and David,
Isaiah and Zachariah, many patriarchs and a throng
      of heroes too,
    a company of prophets, a host of women,
        many virgins,
    a countless multitude of folk, all were baptized
        and redeemed.

In the darkest corner of the doomsday cell
           sat a trinity of figures.
Two were minstrels, Widsith and Dior.
They flanked a still-life figure.
His eyes were closed, the open palm of his right
       hand extended.
He remained removed from the ritual, meditative
       and absorbed,
           perplexed by bleeding in ditches and
              the vicissitudes of time."

(2)

For thirty years, an aged couple, swaddled in rags,
           has trudged from sandy heights
            down the steep hill to the harbor
              at Antifogasta.

With a few pennies they buy fish and flour,
           then turn away from the shores
              where they lost their two sons to the sea.
With their flour and fish,
           they struggle upward to their weather-torn
           house on the hill.

Sent early to sorrow, these same sons were drowned
      at Limnos
           in the Aegean and at Anah in the Euphrates.

A boy with the falling sickness saw a serpent swallow
      the boats.

(3)

The Great Flood

The earliest known forecast of the most famous
   highly-publicized flood
      that covered the world was made by a
         minnow meteorologist.
The tiny fish appeared in a basin in which a plowman
   was washing his hands.
"Keep and protect me, Manu," the minnow pleaded,
      "until I have grown in strength beyond
         destruction
      and can swim in wild waves of the sea,
      and I will save you from the great flood
         that is coming to cover the world."
Caught up by wonder and fear, Manu consented.

The fish had sufficient funds,
      earned at Staples,
         to finance a spacious aquarium and also a
            great ship for Manu.

When waters of the flood began to threaten, Mahara,
   the monster fish,
      towed Manu in his ship to the highest
         northern mountain.

The ship was tied to the trunk of a great protruding tree.
After a number of days (some say forty and that

Manu liked animals)
the waters of the flood receded and Manu, as
promised, was saved.

Anthropologists and explorers, men of faith, shipwrights
and lawyers,
continue to search for Manu's ship and Noah's ark.
Some gurus teach that both are anchored on the
same metaphor.

Manu himself, dazed and helpless,
awakened upon a small island.
He was lonely, without a companion,
believing himself to be the sole survivor of the
flood.

But Karl Jung was wading in shallow waters off
Isabela Island
interviewing minnows.
He wanted to know how a minnow could know
what Noah had learned from External Voices.

Before completing his psychic excursion,
Jung learned that Manu was a Hindu Pygmalion
who kept cows and practiced originating species.
From clarified butter, sour milk,
whey and curds, he had, in one year,
produced a woman destined to become the
Mother of his race.

Jung advised advanced students that Eve
        had become flesh and bone from a rib;
        Galatea from marble;
        and Manu's helpmate from dairy products.

The creators all were well-meaning, reasonable people:
        Jehovah, who went so far as to rely upon
            surgical means
            to provide an "afterthought help meet"
                for his overworked "all alone" boy;
        Aphrodite, passionately bringing breath to
            Pygmalion's sex toy;
        and a Common Sense dreamer, who knew
            he was lonely
                and needed a milkmaid.

(4)

Before the writer of Genesis
        decided, consented, or was inspired
            to roll out his scroll and be the authorized
                spokesman
    for settling once and for all the problem of pairs
        and creation,
he was apparently briefed or familiar with
        arrangements
and rules in the original garden, and had
        chosen friends
            among herdsmen, not vegetarians.

He traveled a lot and had CNN sources.
Esperanto had gone by the boards.
Tongues were confused and wickedness earthquaked
    the nations.
Nobodaddy sent Noah a minnow to warn him and
    build him a boat.
Intentional Design began shopping on E-bay for a
    seaworthy Evinrude.
In brief, it transpired that Makara, the monster fish
    of the Hindus,
        became known as Poseidon in Greece.

Poseidon was not really a fish.
He ruled the waves from his coral palace under the sea.
With his brother, Zeus, he manufactured a deluge
        because Zeus regarded the wickedness of mankind
            distasteful.

After nine days and nights of rain (in some accounts forty),
        the earth, except for the highest peak of Mt.
        Parnassus, was covered.
As the waters rose, Prometheus, wise and ingenious,
            placed his son and niece in a box.
These two floated to the mountain parcel of dry land
    and were saved.

Tellers of tales, as well as box, ship, and ark builders,
        are intrigued by such anachronistic
            similar stories.

Some have sailed with both Darwin and Keats to
   view these indelible,
      changing, repeated interlaced islands of gold.

(5)

Galapagos Neighbors

In the land of the Incas,
      three holy places still abide:
Titicaca, the island of the Sun's appearing;
The Temple of Tiahuanaco;
      and the mountain of the rainbow,
         Huanacauri.
In the flood that covered the world,
      waters circled Huanacauri's heights;
      but never was his tip submerged.
Ayar Auca and his sister-wife Chiclla
      were great drowned stones
      dwelling in the Place of Idols
        at Tiahuanaco.

Ayar Ucho and his sister-wife Rahua
      dwelt with the Sun in darkness
      deep in a cave on Titicaca Island.
When the deluge covered the world,
      all forms retreated to the rocks.
No fish or bird, tree, blade of grass, beast or
   mortal breathed.
All forms were deluged in the soil, locked in stone.
Space alone kept land and water from extinction.

The skies were without stars, sun and moon;
      the universe was darkness.
Space was the Keeper of the Void.

A day of Inti passed.
His spirit moved through chaos in a dream.
The Great Flood ceased.
The island of his refuge rose above the waters.

Ayar Ucho and Rahua lifted Inti from his cavern
      and carried him aloft on condor's wings.
A rainbow circled Huanacauri's peak at their rising.
All day, the strength of condors kept Inti on his
    curving way.

Butterflies they were at evening, weary,
      drifting down in twilight skies
      to sleep in Sutictoco's cave,
      until the dawn of their appearing --
      children, lost, confused and weeping
        in the trees at Pisac.

Ayar Ucho and Rahua were responsible condors.
They carried Inti for a day, without environmental damage
      to any forms that emerged from the flood.

(6)

The Greeks were not so lucky.
Ovid tells the rising-plot story:

Born of an earthly mother,
    Phaethon tried sorting through some
      well-shredded records,
        hired a score of nativity lawyers,
         and learned by the sweat of his brow
          that Helios, the Sun, was his Dad.

With a paternity suit set aside as "no contest,"
    Helios, with great trepidation, allowed the young
      claimant,
    without academy training, to take the reins of
      his chariot
        on a single day's run.

The berserk journey with soon-maddened horses
      was the sound of Much Music –
    brushing, hot-breathed past Leo and Pisces,
    plunging, igniting and scorching the earth in
    numberless places --
    burning good timber, atop Mt. Parnassus,
      even the waterproof box of Prometheus
        built to save his kids from the flood.

Ovid's art was witty, researched, and often prophetic.
In Phaethon's flight he dared to touch on family matters;
    predict world-wide droughts from global warming;
    and offer first hand information for random-target
    video games.

Phaethon's cyclic legacy, happenstance,

               or intentional design

        sent Helios and His Pyromaniac Heir

        to scorch the selfsame sands.

At the sacred Second Coming,

        immorality's maelstrom set Baghdad on fire.

The Charioteer assumed no blame for DUI.

The horses were Arabian,

      the chariot manufactured and insured in Riyadh.

(7)

In contrast to accounts by imitative poets

    whisking sailing vessels to high places

        to avoid extinction from tsunamis,

John Milton spied Satan, in a dry season,

           deceiving Uriel, the angel of the sun,

    to take a foothold in Assyria on top of Mt. Niphates

    and begin his revenge for being thrown out of
Heaven.

The disgraced archangel made the mistake of ignoring

        who begat who,

    and ended by blaspheming his Maker.

He flippantly and seriously claimed not to know

    if he had been made from a rib, stone, or yogurt.

The war that ensued was severe and lengthy,

    the drama embellished by robust blank verse,

    even though the outcome was known some days in
advance.

Milton missed, however, in his blindness,
    an unseen presence in the fray.

On the third day of battle, Messiah himself drove
    his "fierce Chariot"
        to expel the rebel crew:
    "His countenance too severe to be beheld
    And full of wrath bent on his enemies."
The fierce attack was fostered by Satan's Satanic
    "outside the rules"
        employment of artillery:

    "Immediate in a flame,
    But soon obscured with smoke,
        all Heav'n appear'd,
    From those deep-throated engines belcht,
        whose roar
    Embowell'd with outrageous noise the Air,
    And all her entrails tore, disgorging foul
    Thir divilish glut, chain'd Thunderbolts
        and Hail
    Of Iron Globes..."

    Meanwhile, beyond the battle -- justly waged -
    Secure with laptops and binoculars,
    Pentagon spies, swaddled in classified
    Camouflage, viewed the engines
    Set on wheels and visualized

Advancements in the freedom-bringing species
Dwarfing antiquated boiling fat and battering rams:

Smart bombs, flutter bombs, and land mines,
atomic subs and spy planes,
long-range missiles and grenades,
aircraft carriers and destroyers,
phosphorous shells and gases,
agent orange and radiation.

What immortal hand or eye dare frame such
fearful weaponry?

(8)

Whether Matthew, Mark and Luke
sat down together at tea
to compare and edit gospel copy
is an Auden "hard question."
Certainly, all agree they were told they would hear of wars
and rumors of wars, but not to be troubled –
"for these things must needs come to pass."

Supporting his same-caucus comrades
with the Thirty Years War underway,
the Dean of St. Paul's, "No man is an island"
John Donne
fell prey
to the teeth of Leviathan's terror,
coiling in his ancestral pattern
safeguarding war:

"By the benefit of the light of reason,"

        Donne said in his 1621 Christmas sermon,

"Men have found out artillery –

        by which warres come to quicker ends than
        heretofore,

            and the great expense of blood is avoyded:

                for the number of men slain now,

            since the invention of Artillery,

                is much less than before,

        when the sword was the executioner."

(9)

When the Mayflower landed at Plymouth Iraq,

        Bush, Bradford, Columbus, Cortez and Pizarro

    all came properly blessed and appropriately armed.

Arrows of the Pequots and forts of wood and straw

        were temporary obstacles to the Promised Land
        invasion.

Bradford was pleased with the odors rising

           from the Massacre at Mystic River.

The burning bodies of the Pequots were "as incense to
    Jehovah."

The ships of Columbus, Cortez and Pizarro

           were crammed with weapons and slaves,

        missionaries and copies of The Ten Commandments.

Atrocities, starvation, displacements and "the Book"

        prepared the way for "sea-to-sea" salvation.

Maidu natives needed special attention.
They were heretical marvels,
    believing good people at death
    traveled into the Great White Light of the Milky Way,
    and the bad became tumbleweeds and boulders
            awaiting re-incarnation.
(10)
    Freezing in a tent made of rags, lips quivering
        in earthquaked Pakistan,
    A mother and her child
    Huddle together in embers of their everyday lives.

    Driving a tank in Iraq,
        Arlington bound,
        a living Marine prepares for a day
            of late-term abortions.

    Walking through mold and debris
        in beheaded New Orleans,
            a deranged woman
        watches the crescent moon
        shine on bare bones and skulls of Iraqis
            sent by the Aztecs.

    In Lambeth a pondering painter
        sits in the temple of his own mind.
    He did not learn of suffering,
        death and dislocation
        from a voice above the clouds.

He met them in the London streets
        and in the Ghost of a Flea.
The flea he painted is sharp-toothed,
        clawed and human,
        stalking his victims,
      carrying a basin of blood.

This same creature,
      mired to mid-breast in a pool of black ice,
      appeared to Dante Alighieri and Virgil
             in the lowest circle of Hell.

"This is Nimrod, the Mighty Hunter of Mankind," said Virgil.
Breathless, as if suspended between life and death,
      Dante saw a trinity of monstrous faces grown
          upon the torso!
Black waters of Lethe streamed ceaselessly upon them,
      turning to fire in their maws and to ice in the pool.
The foremost face of Freedom's Crusader
         was a fiery embryo of a Mind Left Behind.
Joined to the massive left shoulder,
      torture's defender gurgled behind a mask of black
      flame.
Saturn's hireling, on the right shoulder,
      tongued out in red flame, over and over again,
         the name of each child sent to be swallowed.

Turning to find the passage for their upward journey,
Virgil and Dante wondered aloud if the profligate three
                              would be able to follow:
Be able to walk upon water from Atlanta to Montgomery?
Find fish and loaves to feed the multitudes?
Make salt?
Turn water into wine?

The Circle

I watched my tribe build
>the lodge of the Sun Dance
>when I was eleven.
I heard that the poles
>must be perfectly set,
>for they are the four directions
>that touch at one center.

That was a long time ago.
I know now
>that the tent poles
>are Ezekiel's vision,
>>the four Zoas,
>the four teeth of Tlaloc,
>the four arms of Shiva,
>the four faces of Man,
>the four rivers of Eden.

I know now
>that the poles touch
>at the sun's axle,
>at the still point
>>of the turning world,

at the center
of the gyres,
in the midst
of the wheels
of the cherubim,
at the confluence
of the waters
of Eden.

When I was a child,
I knew the four poles
of our tepee
Held skins to surround
and protect us.

Sarmad the Jew

(Put to death in Mogul India in 1658)

He memorized the Torah early
    and left his native land

To learn the ways and languages
    of far-off people —

Viewed Hindu rituals at Varanasi;

Moslems on their faith-pledged hadj to Mecca;

Corpses without creeds
    abandoned to birds and maggots
        in dust-blown fields.

"I am a Moslem," he declared,
    "when I feel the Koran's power;

But no book tells me all words needful.

Sacred breath, I know, stirs every flower
    rising from the seeds
    of poetry and passion.

No Jew or Hindu, Christian, Buddhist or Parsee
    breathes separate and alone.

All are the instruments of all fulfillments.

We touch each other with our breathing.

We are beauty and wisdom,
    crudity and cruelty.

Turned away from hatred and selfhood,
    we perceive that we are, ourselves,
        the Holy One
    called by many names."

He dared to say such heresies to Aurangzeb
    who took his head.

Puerto Iguazu Madonna

Dust of the road
    and the fields
      is red in the jungle heat
        of Puerto Iquazu.
There, in the cool of morning,
      shaded by sycamore trees,
      the Mother and her Child
        appeared to me,
    carved in white stone,
        coppered by dust,
    fashioned by hands
      from a village
      acquainted with earth.
Sallow and hollow cheeked
    the face of the woman,
      thick-lipped and wide-nostriled.
Flat breast, broad shoulders;
Closed, unfathomable, gentle eyes
    looking at the sleeping child,
          softly held
      with large, bold hands.
Red dust on her fingers,
    shoulders, shut lids,
      and the body of the child.

Clay carved in clay,
   holding dust.
Sunshafts reddening
   through the sycamore trees.
The jungle breeze
   already lifting up
     the edge of heat.
I left her there
   to succour the child
   through long, cicada-sounding nights
   and dust-filled, heat-sick afternoons.
I left her there
   to turn again, in memory,
   to look at her face,
   to ask her to speak
     of tenderness,
     persistence,
     and the dignity of dust.